Yo!
How to Speak
Philadelphian

Yo! How to Speak Philadelphian

by

Claudio Salvucci

MidAtlantica

ISBN 978-1-971738-00-0

*To my fellow Philadelphians
who taught me to speak a dialect that everyone hates,
and to enjoy every minute of it.*

Table of Contents

Innerduction

Americans love to have a good laugh about our regional dialects. I've got a little collection of "folk dictionaries" from the Northeastern US—and nearly all of them have some element of humor in them. We take immense pleasure in piecing out proper dialect pronunciations from spellings like "wooder", "toidy-toid", "dahntahn," and "pahk the cah". And everyone seems fond of the contraction "djeet" (did you eat?) judging by its appearance almost anywhere dialect books are sold.

But until now, there hasn't been a folk dictionary for Philadelphian. Jim Quinn and others have written some great magazine and newspaper articles. Clark DeLeon and Stu Bykofsky have both included Philly glossaries in their books, and Michael Lawrence Ellis has produced a little booklet of Philly Fun-ics. And in the 1990s I wrote a Philadelphian grammar and dictionary as well, but they are hard to find now and were probably not the kind of book most people were looking for anyway.

Linguists haven't always been particularly fond of these kinds of works. And perhaps we can't blame them. After all, they spend their days trying to understand dialects at a serious, technical, detailed level—delving into the minutiae of sounds and making subtle distinctions that most of us laymen don't even know even exist. They take surveys, collect data, and even analyze speech with scientific equipment. And to do this, they use specialized writing systems like the International Phonetic Alphabet. So they have at times gotten understandably frustrated when the subject they discuss at a scholarly level is treated as, well, a joke.

I'm not a linguist, but I very much depend on their work. So I really appreciate all the massive amount of time they've spent studying the weird and wonderful dialect of Philadelphia. And it's because I have such respect for the work of William Labov and others in the field, that I've honestly been a little hesitant to write what could well be taken by some as yet another example of the "Djeet?" school of dialect humor.

But I also have to speak up for the humorists and the writers of folk dictionaries. The way we speak in the United States is too fascinating a subject to be left to a small group of academics. And if the public's perception of their own dialect is to ever get beyond "Djeet?", dialectology is going to have to come down from its academic perch and present its findings in a way that everyone can understand and participate in. That's something that academics have not always succeeded at—but that humorists do phenomenally well.

I've been studying the Philadelphia dialect for 30 years, at all levels from technical linguistics papers to the lowliest humor pieces. And absolutely nothing has dissuaded me from my original conviction that Americans who *speak* a dialect should also have a way to *write* it—whether humorously or any other way. In his *Inquirer* column of May 1, 1983, Clark DeLeon—who probably did more than anyone to actually write Philadelphian—once agreed with a reader Molly Daly of East Falls, who wrote "I wish there were a standardized spelling of the sounds we make...Even with that, I wonder if it would do us justice." I also agree—and I believe that standardization has already been happening under our noses, with native speakers gradually settling on spellings that they tend to like best. A great example is **Fluffya,** which has even earned high praise from no less an expert than William Labov himself.

Serious dialectologists of the 1800s weren't at all ashamed to write **abaout** in their work, and I think that old attitude toward written dialect was much more open-minded—and more in line with the way dialects are treated in other countries—than what was current in the American academy when I started my research. And thankfully, I am starting to see that old open-mindedness come back.

In that spirit, I've tried to bring together the old literary and folk studies with the new scientific data, in order to accurately describe the city's dialect as it is spoken *and written* by Philadelphians. We can realize Molly Daly's wish for a standardized written Philadelphian, by respecting some of the common conventions that Clark DeLeon and others have already established, such as **wooder**, **iggle**, and **Fluffya**. To those conventions we can also add our own particular preferences as native speakers, as I've done throughout this book.

I've tried to describe the classic dialect that I heard and spoke in the Far Northeast in the 1970s and the 80s. But language moves on, just as we ourselves do, and it's been more than a decade now since I've even lived in the Delaware Valley. So while I wouldn't dare claim to be a good source for the latest "jawn" era of Philadelphia speech, I hope at least to document a moment in time that some of us still fondly remember in the City of Brotherly Love.

—Claudio R. Salvucci, Feb. 2026

Da Phulladulphia Accent

Philadelphia has an accent all its own—a unique combination of sounds that is not found anywhere else in the English-speaking world. Oh sure, you might find there the same distinctive **o** in Baltimore and Pittsburgh, a similar **aw** in New York, the **aow** of the South, the common **r** retention of General American, and the same **youse**, **dem** and **dose** of other Northeastern and Midwestern cities.

But what makes Philadelphia distinctive is not necessarily any of these individual pronunciations. It's the whole *pattern*: how Northeastern, Midland, and Southern pronunciations have blended together in a unique way. That overall pattern is what allows us natives to hear a very familiar intonation in some faraway state or nation, and say: "Wait...are you from Philly?"

In this section we will look at all the various sound changes that make up the overall Philly accent. And, in the process, we'll also have occasion to review some of the different ways people have tried to represent those sounds on paper.

The Philadelphia o

One of our most notable sounds is what linguists call our fronted long **o** heard in words like **home, phone,** and **boat**. Instead of starting it with a normal **o** sound and ending with **oo**, like "oh-oo", we start out with the short **e** of **bet**. So we say something like "eh-oo" in long **o** words: "heh-oom", "pheh-oon", "beh-oot."

As distinctive and classically Philadelphian as it is, this sound is a tough one to get on paper. Strictly speaking it isn't critical to spell it differently, as it's really just a slight variation on the normal long **o**. But that hasn't stopped people from trying. In the 20th century variations of **ao** were common, like **nao** (no), **hellaow** (hello), **raoad** (road). But more recently people have tended to use **ew**: **hewm** (home), **phewn** (phone), **hewgie** (hoagie).

The Two Kinds of Short a

Few things in the Philadelphia accent are as complicated as the way we pronounce short **a**. There have even been linguistics papers written about how hard it is for outsiders who move to Philly to learn our system.

Like many areas of the country now, Philadelphians have two kinds of short **a**. One of them is the standard sound of **cat** and **bat**—this is called "lax a". The other one is a nasal variation that sounds a lot like the vowel in **air**—this is called "tense a". Jim Quinn noted in his 1976 article that in Philadelphia the two names Ann and Ian sound the same: "ee-yan".

Tense short **a** is another hard sound to capture on paper. Personally, I like to spell tense **a** with an **ae**, because that way it doesn't get confused with anything else, but other variations are also common, such as **aa**.

The tense short **a** appears before certain sounds like **f**, **n**, **m**, **s**, and hard **th**: **haef** (half), **Aenn** (Ann), **haem** (ham), **paess** (pass), and **baeth** (bath). That's not too hard of a rule, right? Well, here's where it starts to get crazy. Because Philadelphians don't apply this general rule so simply. So **swam**, **began**, and **math** have lax **a**. And though short **a** before **d** is generally lax (e.g., **Chad**, **dad**, **fad**, **had**, **lad**, **pad**, **rad**, **sad**, **tad**), it's tense in three specific words: **maed** (mad), **baed** (bad), **glaed** (glad). Other words, like **ran,** seem to go either way—at least the way I say it. But maybe I'm just linguistically muddled at this point.

The difference between tense and lax **a** can even give you two different words. Lax **madder** is the standard word "matter", and tense **maedder** is the comparative of **mad**: "more mad." Even though the noun **caen** is tense, the verb **can** "to be able to" is lax. But make that verb a negative and it suddenly becomes tense again and reverses the meaning. In Philadelphia, **I caen' do it** means the exact opposite of **I can do it**, and because the **t** was dropped, all that really changes is the quality of the short **a**. Somehow we keep all of this straight without even thinking about it. Pretty impressive!

Pork the Cor on Morkit

This is one of the classic Philadelphian sound changes, and one of the very oldest, as it was already firmly established by the mid-1800s. We take the "ahr" sounds in park, car, and market, and turn them all into "oh-r": **pork**, **core**, **morkit**.

Most of the time this sound has been written with **or**—not only in Philadelphian but also in Baltimorese, which shares this same pronunciation. The only problem with that spelling, though, is that when we Philadelphians see **or**, that triggers in our brains another related change that turns the **or** sound into **oor** (we'll get to that next). This **or** > **oor** change makes it hard for a Philadelphian to see **core** on the page and not say "coor." So, even though it'd be quite accurate for non-Philadelphians to say that we **pork the core on Morket**—that's how it sounds to them—it might be difficult for a native Philadelphian to read that sentence correctly without going one sound change too far and, nonsensically, "poorking the coor on Moorkit." For that reason, I kinda like the spellings **awr** and **aur**: **paurk the caur on Maurket**. It's less common and a little clumsier, but at least when I read it I naturally use the correct sound and am not tempted to say **-oor.**

You Sure Abaout the Shoor?

The way Philly handles long **o** before **r** has sometimes been misunderstood. I've seen this described as a bit of Western lingo imported to Philadelphia: where **sure** becomes **shore**. That's partially correct—there's no question that these two words sound the same locally. But the change actually goes in the opposite direction: we take words that started out with **or** "oh-r" sounds, and push them into the **oor/ure** "oo-r" category. So we take a **toor** of the neighborhood and we vacation **daowna shoor**.

So between this change and the "pork the cor on Morket" mentioned above, travelers to Philly have a lot to keep straight. They have to remember that **stors** twinkle in the night sky and **stoores** sell things; a **cor** is what you drive and a **coor** is the center of an apple. **Por** and **scoore** you might hear on a golf course; but **poor** and **scor** you might see on your skin. **for** is the opposite of near, **foor** is one more than three.

Haow ta Pronaounce Daowntaown

One of the most long-standing characteristics of the Philadelphia dialect is our "ow" in words like **down**. In standard American English, this sound typically starts with the broad **a** of **father** gliding into long **u**, giving the sound "ah-oo". But since the mid-1800s, Philadelphians have started it not with broad **a** but with the short **a** of **cat** or even, in extreme cases, the **ai** of **air**: "ă-oo" or "ai-oo." This change of course is common in the South and is part of what gives the Philadelphia accent its quasi-Southern sound. It probably crept into our speech as we started vacationing on the Jersey Shore: **aow** is even older in South Jersey than it is in Philadelphia, and was noticed in Cape May by Benjamin Franklin all the way back in 1739 (see page 21).

Since this pronunciation was first observed, it has been common to use **aou** and **aow** to write it. This three letter combination works well in almost every situation and is commonly used in other dialects as well. Occasionally one also sees longer two-syllable variations like **hay-ouse**. More recently, however, **al** or even **ail** are being used: **al** (ow), **salth** (south). Michael Lawrence Ellis gives a great example of a sentence that, on paper, doesn't look like it could possibly make sense—until you actually try to read it with a Philadelphia accent: **Hail nail braille'n kale?** for **How now brown cow?**

How does that beautiful mess actually work? As we've already said, the nucleus of the "ow" sound can go as high as the **ai** of **air**—so the vowel is right where it is supposed to be. And **l** in Philadelphia is heavily vocalized and pronounced so far back in the mouth that it comes close to the glide in **ow/ou** (merging **pow** and **pal**, **bounce** and **balance**—more on that in the section on **l** below).

As remarkably as this spelling trick works in this sentence though, there are too many problems with it to use generally. It is too easy to pronounce **al** as "awl" in some contexts. For example, if we tried to write **aout** as *****alt**, it looks like it should be read as "awl-t", not "ă-oot". So while there certainly are applications where the **al** spelling works brilliantly like **salth**, **aou/aow** works in more contexts and is more reliable. The other trouble is (if we care) using **al** spellings for **ow** is not good at showing *other* people how we speak; if you pronounce a standard **l** instead of dark **l** then your **salth** may not come out sounding very Philadelphian (or understandable) at all.

The Race for Mare

Words with **-ayor** get simplified to **-are**. So you will commonly hear the word **mayor**, for example, turned into a one-syllable word: **mare** (mayor), **pare** (payor). This also applies to compounds, so the four-syllable **mayoralty** becomes the three-syllable **marelty**.

A Plegg of Beggles, a Lig of Iggles

The long *a* sound gets flattened out to short *e* when it occurs before *g*. So in Philadelphia we get **beggle** (bagel), **vegg** (vague), **plegg** (plague). Long *e* before *g* also gets flattened: *lig* (league), *iggle* (eagle), *illiggle* (illegal).

Cawfee Tawk

We Philadelphians love our *aw* sound almost as much as Noo Yawkas. We tend not to draw it out so long or add it to our *chawklit*—that's just plain old *chocklit* to us—but we love to sit and *tawk* over *lawng* sips of *cawfee awn* a cold day. And also like New York, we keep our *cot* and our *caught* sounds very far apart and don't merge them at all, unlike our neighbors from Scranton and from Western Pennsylvania (and indeed, most of the Western half of the country).

Furry Crawss ta Jurzy

Words with -*erry* end in -*urry* in Philadelphia, with the short *e* vowel turning into a short *u*. So Philadelphians wish each other a **Murry Chrissmiss** and give their kids gifts if they are **vurry** good. We take the *furry* to Camden Aquarium. Linguistics research has shown that this change is pretty well restricted to the city of Philadelphia itself, and that it doesn't reach very far into the outlying suburbs. So it's one of the few sound changes that is quite unique to Philadelphia proper.

An unstressed schwa before *r* also tends to be pushed farther back—so the first vowel in "Jersey," instead of being pronounced at the front or the middle of the mouth, goes all the way to the back. Since this is a slight variation, there's no real need to represent it in written dialect, although to my ear (and eye!), writing **Jurzy** just feels more authentically Philadelphian somehow.

Tull 'em ta Spull Dullaware

We take the **furry** across the **Dullaware** of course, because we also do the same with short **e** before **l**. We take the **ullavater**, see **ullaphints** at the Zoo, and **tull** people we live in **Phulladulphia,** however it might be **spulled**. An easy switch from **e** to **u** in the spelling will work most of the time here, but it might sometimes be necessary to add an **h** when we write this sound, so we can tell the difference between the animal **bull** (with the vowel of **pull**) and the Liberty **Buhll** (with the vowel of **dull**).

Graddytude: a Beautyful Addytude

One of the classic pronunciations that you'll almost always see mentioned is the long **e** that many of us put in the middle of words like **beautyful**, **addytude**, **graddytude**. This same change is reported, though less commonly, in other contexts and words such as **gratyfy**, **mortyfy**, and **multyply**. And there seems to be considerable local variation as well: Philadelphians may say both **indypendence** and **innapennense**.

Huyst and Hooyst are not Aluyk

Long **i** splits into two different sounds in Philadelphian. One is the standard long **i**, pronounced "ah-ee": we'll use that in words like **fly**, **time**, **hide**, and **alive**. But we also have another variation pronounced "uh-ee" that starts not with the **ah** of **father** but with the **uh** of **cup**.

This variation is called a "raised long *i*", and it is heard when long *i* is followed by *p*, *t*, *k*, or *s* sounds, in words like *pipe*, *fight*, *bike*, *ice*, and *heist*. Very rarely it even occurs at the end of a word, like the *i* in *high school*, and we seem to say *spuyder* (spider) for some reason.

During a Flyers game you might have heard announcers say "Fluh-yers" and "he fuh-yers the puck"—that's called Canadian raising and it's basically the same sound, although Canadians use it in a lot more words than we do. It's also common in Ireland—in fact we may well have gotten it from the Irish (Uyrish) who came to Philadelphia in the 1800s. And maybe New Yorkers got it from them too; the old stereotypical Brooklynese phrase *soive the ersters* was for most speakers actually *suyve the uysters*, with "uh-ee", not "oh-ee". So raised long *i* is a pretty common sound in English, though different regions use it in different ways and different contexts.

Most people have tended to approximate the "uh-ee" sound in Philadelphian and other dialects with *oi*, writing *poip*, *foit*, *boik*. But in our dialect it's not at all the same sound as *oi*: *heist* and *hoist* sound very different. That's why I like to use *uy*, which has also been used by Sean Monahan and in traditional New York dialect. Although it may look rather confusing and unfamiliar the first time you see it, I think it works much better in the long run. You *muyt fuyt* me on spellings of that *tuyp*, but I'll keep *ruyt* on using them unless something better comes down the *puyk*.

Awl Rol'd up Abaout Ahrn

Before *l*, the standard long *i* loses its *y* sound (also called the glide), going from "ah-ee" to just plain "ah". This is characteristic of Southern dialects, and Pennsylvania traditionally marks the northern limit of this change along the East Coast, where it does indeed occur but only in limited contexts.

You could easily spell it with **ah**, which is what Southern dialect writers typically use. However, Philadelphians and Baltimoreans alike seem to prefer the **o** look on this. So there might be a 10 car **pol-up** for half a **mol**, but don't get **rol'd** up, and keep track of your **mollage**.

Some Philadelphians also seem to show glide deletion before **r**: **fahr** (fire), **tahr** (tire). None of the eight Philadelphians in the 1939 survey showed it, yet there were scattered people in the suburban counties who did. R. Whitney Tucker said he heard it among moderately well-educated people in Delco in 1944, and Bill Labov attributes it to many Philadelphians in a 2006 interview for the *Daily Pennsylvanian*.

However, Philadelphians often object to spellings like **arn** (iron). I did for a long time too—**arn** certainly doesn't seem natural to my speech, and I doubted I even had any glide deletion until I paid closer attention and realized I said **tahrd** (tired). Checking the Philly-area speakers on the *International Dialects of English Archive*, they pronounced the glide in "tire" when reading a written text, but they also show glide weaking or dropping in **retahred** (retired). In one case there is a strong **Ahrland** (Ireland) in unscripted speech.

I think what is going on here is that Philadelphians may well drop the glide in **ire**, but we tend to reject the **ar** spelling for a very good reason. Importantly, Tucker points out that when the glide is lost in Philadelphia, **fire** becomes **fahr** [faːr], which is then kept distinct from the backed **ar** in words like **faur** (*far*), phonetically [fɔːr]. The former starts on the broad **a** of **father**, whereas the latter starts on the **aw** of **law**. So in spoken Philadelphian, even if we delete the glide we wouldn't confuse **Bahrn** (Byron) with **baurn** (barn). This is a critical distinction and is probably why some Philadelphians object to **iron** written as *arn;* it would have to be something like **ahrn** instead. Note, however, that **ire** and **ar** *do* actually merge in nearby areas, like the New Jersey Pinelands, the Delmarva Peninsula, southcentral Pennsylvania, and Maryland. Indeed, Kurath and McDavid called this merger "a characteristic feature of Midland speech." So it is very possible to hear it in the area.

Wur the L is Ciddy Haw in Fluffya?

Philadelphians generally pronounce **l** by raising their tongues at the back of the mouth—instead of using the tip of the tongue against the teeth, as most Americans do. This variation is called "dark l". In fact, in some Philadelphians, dark **l** is also pronounced with a rounding of the lips—called "vocalization"—that almost makes the **l** indistinguishable from a **w** or can even make it disappear entirely: **Ciddy Haw** (City Hall), **Wahwood** (Wildwood), and the *-uff-* for *-elph-* in **Fluffya**. Sometimes you will see this dark **l** spelled with a **g**, such as in Jim Quinn's example of "glorious gargle": **Gliddle gluglu glives in glillilly** (Little Lulu lives in Little Italy).

Yur Booy is Hooystin His Ooy's

The **oi** sound doesn't escape the Philadelphia treatment. Typically it starts with the **aw** of **law**: "aw-ee." But we start it further forward in the mouth with the long **u** of **too**: "oo-ee". A **booy** might need **ooyl** for his **tooy** truck if the **hooyst** gets stuck. Note though that **booy** does not rhyme with **buoy**, which is two syllables, more like "bewey."

A Haen if Yizz Unnerstaen

The **d** sound tends to drop out completely after **n**, especially in final position **haen** (hand), **unnerstaen** (understand). But it doesn't happen in every single environment. At least the way I speak, I don't do this in blender, fender, and lender.

Winner in Cenner City

Something very similar happens with the **t** sound. So we might wanna **enner** a contest or go to **Cenner City**. If you slide on **winner** ice, you might get your **rennal** car **dennid**.

But unlike with **d**, we don't tend to drop **t** at the end of words, so you can still hear it at the end of words like **ant**, **want**, **dent**, **rent**.

Shtring Baens aun Broad Shtreet

A funny thing happens to **str** words in Philly: the first part turns from a plain old **s** to an **sh** sound. So drive **shtraight** on Broad **Shtreet** and stay within the **shtruyps**—unless of course, you're in a **shtring baend**, in which case **shtrum** and **shtrut** away!

Wich Withaout a Wisper

Many Americans once pronounced **w** and **wh** differently—and a few still do. They pronounce **wh** with a whisper, like trying to say **w** and **h** at the same time. So **wheat**, **whip**, and **which** come out "hweat', "hwip", "hwich".

Philadelphians haven't made any distinction between those two sounds for a long, long time. Our lack of **wh** goes back to colonial times, and it is the first distinctive Philadelphia pronunciation we have evidence of. Perhaps it was even Philadelphia's lead that inspired the simplification of this sound nationwide, as in modern American English this distinction is mostly gone.

Save Wauder, Drink Wooder

Our pronunciation of **wooder** for "water" has become famous — and we've tended to really latch onto it as a classic Philadelphianism. This spelling first appeared in a reader's letter to the *Inquirer* as early as 1972—but Philadelphians have differed on this, and there have been other spellings offered like **wauder**, **warter**, and even **wutter**.

Bert Vaux's survey shows that Philadelphians are split on how to being the word **quarter**: with a **kw** sound or with a **k** sound alone. My pronunciation is **quooder**, and I suspect that those who leave off the **w** sound pronounce it **corter** (I can't imagine that anyone says "cooder", to rhyme with **do-gooder**).

Yumor

Another place where **h** disappears is in words like **human**, **humid**, and **humor**. Traditionally these pronounced with an **h+y** sound, but in Philadelphia just the **y** remains, so we get **yumin**, **yumid**, and **yumor**.

Fuyt'n Wurds

Professor William Labov (1927-2024) of the University of Pennsylvania, an expert on the scientific analysis of Philadelphia pronunciation, designed a test to find out if Philadelphians could distinguish certain words. One person would read a word out loud. A second person, who couldn't see the word, had to guess what the other person was reading. The test proved remarkably successful in showing that many Philadelphians couldn't hear any difference between the two words.

It also proved remarkably successful in starting fistfights between the participants. Labov eventually had to call it off.

Here are some examples of word pairs that many Philadelphians pronounce exactly the same. But please, for your own safety—don't try the test at home.

merry	Murray
ferry	furry
bounce	balance
cowrie	calorie
Powell	pal
Mayor	mare
mirror	mere
pore	poor
shore	sure
tore	tour

Phulladulphia Grammur

Although Philadelphians generally use the same English grammar as most other Americans, our dialect shows a few strange constructions that can sound very unnatural to others but quite natural and normal to us. Granted, most of these aren't **only** used in Philadelphia—they tend to be more regional than strictly local—but even if you work on getting rid of your accent, some of these might accidentally give you away without you even knowing it.

Youse

The English language lost a separate word for plural **you** centuries ago—and it doesn't seem to have ever gotten over the loss, because it keeps trying to put one back in. Like many other urban areas in the northern U.S., Philadelphia has **youse** or **yuze** to refer to two or more people in the second person. Often you might hear this in an unstressed form that sounds more like **yizz**: **Aur yizz gehwin**?

And in practice, the two forms are often used in the singular as well. Clark DeLeon noted in his column of August 8th, 1987: "In case you're wondering, the plural of yuze is yiz. But yuze won't be wrong if yuze usem interchangeably."

Youse is heavily stigmatized, so its usage has tended to decline in favor of the more generally accepted **you guys**.

Anymore is Positive Anymore

In most English dialects, you can generally only use the word "anymore" together with a negative, as in: **We don't do that anymore**. But in Philadelphia and the Midland dialect areas of the Midwest, it is widely accepted for people to use it without the negative, in sentences like **We still do that anymore**, or **Things are so expensive anymore**. This usage is called "positive anymore", and in context, it means something like "nowadays" or "currently".

You Done this Book Yet?

I have to admit, I'm *still* stunned that "done" followed by a direct object without any preposition isn't acceptable in some people's dialects. It's engrained so deeply in my speech pattern I had no idea there was even any question about it, but my Long Islander wife and my Northeastern Pennsylvania kids still insist that it's flat-out wrong. Maybe they're just not done their homework.

Ye Olde Philly Addytude

Philadelphians' way of speaking has been confusing, confounding, and irritating the rest of America since Colonial times. Our local dialect has changed a great deal within the last three centuries; you'll see that a few features mentioned below are long gone from our speech pattern now. But one thing that hasn't really changed is how people have reacted to hearing us speak. Here are some of my favorite historical examples.

1739

"...when a Pensilvanian would say PANTHER he shall say PAINTER. When a New Yorker thinks to say (This) he shall say (Diss) and the people in New England and Cape May will not be able to say (Cow) for their Lives, but will be forc'd to say (Keow) by a certain involuntary Twist in the Root of their Tongues."

—Benjamin Franklin, from "Poor Richard's Almanac"

1789

"In the middle states also, many people pronounce a **t** at the end of **once** and **twice**, **oncet** and **twicet**. This gross impropriety would not be mentioned, but for its prevalence among a class of very well educated people; particularly in Philadelphia and Baltimore."

—Noah Webster. Dissertations on the English Language, page 111.

1810

"Who now can hear any thing of the sound of **h** in a numerous class of words when pronounced by a Philadelphian? The words **what, when, where, wheel, which, wharf**, and a hundred others, are pronounced by the unlearned, and alas ! by the learned, exactly thus, **wat, wen, were, weel, witch, warf**, &.C.".

—*Piomingo. The Savage, page 35.*

1826

The dialect of the citizens, particularly of the children…is very defective, and the young misses are detestably affected in their manners, dress and dialect… They have, withal, a whining tone in their speech, extremely disgusting; though the higher classes pronounce the English language with purity and even elegance."

—*Anne Royall. Sketches of History, Life, and Manners, in the United States.*

1868

The Philadelphian accent, which prevails among the oldest and most respectable families as well as among the middle classes, is as peculiar in its way as that of the Southerner…Some of its noticeable features are: the use of **me** for **my**, as in "me own," "me sister," etc., recalling Hibernia; pronouncing **says saays**, instead of **sez**, and **said sayed**, instead of **sed**; converting **Julia** into **Julier**, and **America** into **Ameriker** ; and in such words as **round, pound, down**, etc., imitating the broad twang of the Yankee dialect, by saying **paöund, daöwn**, etc.…

I know of a case where an English nobleman was quite captivated at first sight with a young lady belonging to the "first circles" of Philadelphia, but who was disenchanted when he discovered her use of localisms, and said to a friend subsequently, "She is beautiful as a houri; her loveliness almost bewitched me; but I could never marry *an ignoramus*."

—*Wirt Sykes. "About Philadelphia", in the Northern Monthly Magazine, January 1868.*

"What's the matter with Philadelphians?" asked Muriel. "Are n't they nice?"

"They are not precisely nasty, which is the English alternative, I believe," said Ralph laughing; "but they're so very, so very — Philadelphian! They have a language of their own, and they insist upon talking it before persons who are not used to it. They even defend it, and say it is correct; or else they are unconscious of it, which is more exasperating still."

"Do they really speak a separate language?" asked Muriel, looking very puzzled and serious.

"It is not exactly a language. It's a dialect; which should not astonish you, Miss CarrWynstede, coming from the land of dialects. I'll tell you what I mean. They have a queer way of behaving with their vowels. They eliminate the broad **a** from their speech almost entirely. They say **paaas** and **graaas** and **paaath**. They call chicken, **chickn**, and Ellen, **Elln**, and brown, **brayown**, and **bird**, and **girl** — no! you must hear a Philadelphian 'pur sang' pronounce those words; I could not do justice to them. ...

"When I was at Newport once, before I was married," said Mrs. Bowdoin, "there was a Philadelphian quite devoted to me, who was by way of being a poet....this gentleman invited me one day to go to walk with him on the cliffs, and as we walked he asked if he might repeat a little poem (he called it *poum*) which he had written. I begged him to do so. It began —

'Angel faces haaant mee pillah —'

This is all I can remember, for I was trying so hard not to laugh at the first line, I could not listen to the rest."

—Annie Fields. 1887. A Week Away from Time.

The Luckless Linguist
by Norman Jefferies

A linguist of renown was he,
 In divers tongues he'd speak;
Chinese to him was A B C;
 He said his prayers in Greek.
    In ancient Norse
    He could discourse—
He'd learned it in a week.

Magazine tales in dialect
 He found as clear as day.
In Choctaw he was quite correct,
 His Sanscrit was au fait.
    His gift of gab
    In foreign blab
He'd frequently display.

But, after all, his boast and pride
 Was English undefiled,
A tongue to which he had applied
 Himself when but a child.
    There is no word
    You ever heard
But in his brain was filed.

This sage to Philadelphia came—
 He meant to settle here—
But straight his head bent low with shame,
 For on his startled ear
    Strange sounds there broke.
    His neighbors spoke
A language new and queer!

He knew all tongues, alive or dead;
 Some with age were tainted;
But when a stranger to him said:
 "**Wheresmehat**?" he fainted.
    Moreover "**tork**"
    Of "**Fairmount Pork**"
Dazed this savant sainted.

People, when too tired to "**wark it**,"
 Rode in a "**trolley-core**;"
"**Baaskets**" housewives took to "**moreket**,"
And "**bort**" whate'er they "**sore**."
    For "**corepets noo**"
    They paid when "**doo**"
Their "**dollurs**" by the score.

When "**aasked**" to "**hev**" a "**glaas**" of beer,
 He blinked with mild surprise;
When told to "**set deown**" in a "**cheer**,"
 He puzzled was likewise.
    "**Where is it at?**"
    And – "**it ain't that**"
Brought wonder to his eyes.

* * * * *

Far from the crowd's ignoble strife
 A quiet asylum stands,
And there a linguist booked for life
 In anguish wrings his hands.
    And words he speaks,
    Between his shrieks,
That no man understands.

—*Seen and Heard, Louis N. Megargee, Publisher.*
January 23, 1901.

1909

Philadelphian Wants Scrapple

And from Philadelphia came this message:

"Ask head waiter at leading hotel be sure arrange to serve scrapple two meals for party six."

The village operator again appealed to Louisville:

"What's scrapple?" he asked.

The laugh in Louisville could almost be heard over the wire.

"Must be Philadelphia dialect for something to eat," was the reply. "Fix them a can of sardines."

—*St. Louis Dispatch 2-12-1909, p. 16*

1912

Philadelphia's English

"Some days ago a Press editorial said that the best English spoken was the Philadelphia English. Now this sounds funny to the writer, and he would like to know where in Philadelphia the editor hears it. To an outsider the Philadelphia twang sounds about the worst on earth."

—*The Penn Germania, Feb. 1912*

1936

Philadelphia Accent

"...but meanwhile Texans may take what comfort they can from the fact that a college drama director has broken into the public prints with the unequivocal declaration that Philadelphians have the worst accent in the United States. This lady, who hails from New Haven, Connecticut, says her pupils in Philadelphia do not pronounce vowels correctly but throw them from the back of their mouths and, to her way of thinking, the effect is rather horrible."

—*McAllen Daily Monitor, McAllen, TX March 6, 1936*

Araoun' the Dullaware Valley

Just like American English is not one monolithic dialect, but a collection of different dialects, the Delaware Valley dialect is an abstraction of different speech patterns that we find in the region. We've already mentioned how **vurry** (very), is pretty restricted to the city and not generally found outside of it. But of course, plenty of people have moved from the city out to the suburbs, and vice versa— so the boundaries can't be as cut and dry as the city lines.

Even within the population that speaks the Philadelphia dialect as I've defined it here, we can see some geographical variation. Studies show that the following areas in the Delaware Valley have generally shared the same pattern as Philadelphia, though sometimes with their own unique twists.

First we need to recognize that some of the differences may be ethnic. As we saw in the previous chapter, Irish features like **me hat** predominated in the mid-1800s, and presumably were more heavily concentrated in Irish neighborhoods. Today, many black Philadelphians don't use many of the pronunciation features described here, preferring a black English dialect. Various sources claim that South Philly has an accent all its own that shares some features with the New York dialect, which might be due to South Philly residents adopting some of the speech patterns of Italian Americans there. Yet nearly everyone uses Philly vocabulary like **hoagie**. Ethnic allegiance can certainly affect a person's dialect, but these variations are not geographical so they are beyond the real scope of this book.

The Neighborhoods

Even outside of ethnic differences, there still are subtle linguistic differences between Philly neighborhoods. There just haven't been too many studies investigating the question. Thankfully, we have some good information for the mid-20th century thanks to Dennis Stanley Lebofsky's doctoral thesis, *The Lexicon of the Philadelphia Metropolitan Area* (1970), a veritable linguistic atlas of the city. Here are a few of his findings that showed clear neighborhood distinctions in the mid-1960s:

garreter (gossiper): widespread except Northeast and Northwest

buttonball (sycamore): North Philly, Northeast, and Northwest

leaves out (lets out): North Philly, Kensington

wifty: West Philly, Southwest, Manayunk

tellypole: (telephone pole) mainly Kensington, scattered elsewhere

wallball: western half of city

Southeastern Pennsylvania

The four suburban counties of Bucks, Montgomery, Delaware, and Chester have all been speaking Philadelphian for a long time; they were very clearly aligned with the city in the 1939 data collected for the LAMSAS project. But they have also tended to hold on to rural and other terms that the city eventually lost. Around 1940, some folks in the suburbs were still tending to say *fahr* for fire and *wahr* for wire, and R. Whitney Tucker reported these pronunciations even among the educated in Delaware County. More recently, the Cambridge Survey found *yuge* and *yuman* still reported at the eastern border of Delaware County but otherwise appears largely gone from the suburbs.

Ground hacky was an old Philly term for the chipmunk in the 1800s. By 1965, only one Philadelphian (a 93 year old) still remembered it, but a quarter of the suburbanites knew it, including all three Bucks Countians (aged 75, 55, and 42). Likewise, Chester County shared some expressions with Lancaster County and the lower Susquehanna, like **whicker** for a horse's whinny, and the cow calls **sook/sookie** and **woo/wookie**. People in Bucks and Montgomery counties were still calling cows in the pasture with **co**. Expressions like these died out though as the area modernized and more city-born people moved out to the suburbs.

Although both **crayfish** and **crawfish** have mixed usage throughout Southeastern PA, **crayfish** tends to predominate in the north (Bucks and Montgomery counties), and **crawfish** and **crawdad** are most common to the south and west. One uniquely suburban term that is still holding on is Norristown's **zep**, for a local sandwich similar to a hoagie.

And then of course, there are all the terms common to Pennsylvania that aren't common in New Jersey or Delaware, like **state store** for **liquor store**.

Trenton and Central Jersey

Trenton and its environs are mostly Philadelphian, but also close enough to New York to be affected by its dialect. For example, Trenton has a short **a** system that's halfway between New York and Philadelphia, sharing New York's tense a before **d**: **aedd** (add) but also sharing Philly's lax **a** before **g**: **bag** and **tag**. The **h-** is not dropped in **huge** and **humor**. Central Jersey and the northern part of the shore seem to not generally accept **done your homework** as grammatical, even though it is widely accepted in South Jersey, the Philadelphia suburbs, the Lehigh Valley, and Delaware.

The night before Halloween was called **Tick-Tack Night**, and though Trenton generally prefers Philadelphia's **jimmies** for the candies that are sprinkled on ice cream, it also has its own term for them: **ice cream mints**. And of course Trenton is proud of its native dishes **tomato pie** and **pork roll**. In the mid-1900s, Central Jersey preferred the Northern terms **pail** and **brook** while the Pennsylvania counties preferred **bucket** and **creek**, though usage admittedly seems mixed. **Hoagie** is the preferred term in Trenton and in southern Hunterdon County, but Princeton is divided (with **sub** perhaps the slight leader). Northeast of Princeton **sub** and **deli sandwich** are preferred. Central Jersey also shows divided usage between Philadelphia's **wait in line** and New York's **wait on line**.

Suburban South Jersey

The linguistic influence of Philadelphia has been spreading rapidly with the growth of the suburbs in South Jersey. This expansion has been at the expense of the native Down Jersey dialect—which is discussed later on. New Jerseyans are more familiar than Pennsylvanians with **jughandles**, short off-ramps for making lefts on divided highways, and Joshua Katz's survey shows that South Jersey prefers **crawdad** over **crayfish**.

Jersey Shore

Originally, the Jersey Shore almost certainly shared the Down Jersey/Pine Barrens dialect that was common to the southern half of the state. But that seems to have changed in the mid-1800s when train lines opened up the area to vacationing Philadelphians. By the 1930s, the speech of Atlantic City and the shore was solidly Philadelphian, while interior South Jersey still kept its original Down Jersey speech patterns.

Today, the shore's most famous local term is **shoebie**, a word for the hapless summer tourist from Long Beach Island south. (At Seaside Heights and further north, there's a different word for tourist: **benny**). Although **salt water taffy** is now commercialized and widespread, the term originated in Atlantic City, where many of its leading manufacturers still reside.

Wilmington and Northern Delaware

In Wilmington and Northern Delaware, **-air** is often pronounced **-ur**: **thur** (there), **wur** (where), **Dullawur** (Delaware); this is a feature shared with the Delmarva dialect. Wilmington generally shares the Philadelphia short **a** system, but New Castle residents prefer tense vowels in **raen** (ran), **swaem** (swam), and **begaen** (began).

Wilmingtonians know about **hoagie** but prefer **sub**. Finally, Delawareans are absolutely adamant about going to the **beach** in summer, never the **shore**. So much so, in fact, that in 2003 the legislature passed a resolution that the phrase **shore points**, "while perfectly good English, happens to be alien to the traditions of the First State". An amusingly unrestrained editorial in the *Wilmington News Journal* at the time minced no words in calling **shore points** "New Jersey-Philly jibberish".

Finally, we should also mention that Elkton and Cecil County in Maryland have traditionally been classified as part of the Philadelphia dialect region along with Northern Delaware. This allegiance seems generally borne out by the recent Cambridge online surveys.

Aout Paest da Boorders

Because of multiple dialect surveys from the middle 1900s on, we have a pretty good idea of where the borders of the dialect are, and what is on the other side of those borders. The areas listed below showed enough divergences from Philadelphia—at least historically— to be considered different dialects, though nowadays there may be less differences because of population movement.

Kurath and McGrath defined a large Susquehanna Valley speech area that went from the Lehigh Valley area all the way to central PA, but there are enough differences between the metropolitan areas to warrant looking at them separately. For more recent data, I have used the data collected by the Cambridge Online Survey of World Englishes, run by Bert Vaux and Marius L. Jøhndal.

Allentown-Bethlehem and Reading

The 1939 data shows a very clear demarcation between the classically Philadelphian Bucks and Montgomery Counties and the Pennsylvania Dutch-influenced Lehigh and Northampton Counties. Together with Reading, the Lehigh Valley showed Pennsylvania German-style monophthongal vowels and lacked three key Philadelphia changes: **aow**, fronted long **o**, and **au**. Easton, interestingly, stood somewhat apart and agreed more with Philadelphia. A review of recent discussions online suggests that the old Dutch-style pronunciations are not heard much in the area anymore. But there are still key differences between the Lehigh and Delaware Valleys.

Allentown shows a continuous short *a* system, where the tensest short *a*'s are before *n* and *m* and the laxest are before *p*, *t*, and *k*— with a gradual transition in between. Some Allentown speakers also show the **fool-full** merger mentioned under Harrisburg below, and the area is "transitional" for the **cot-caught** merger. The **day > dee** change in the days of the week, e.g. Philadelphia's **Mundy** and **Tuesdy**, seems to be absent in the Lehigh Valley.

The city of Reading used to belong squarely with the PA Dutch areas, but lately it has adopted more Philadelphia features, like the complex short *a* system. A few speakers in the area do use the Philadelphian **Mundy**, though it still is a minority.

Historically a number of Pennsylvania German terms were once common in the Lehigh Valley, such as **ponhaws** for scrapple, **toot** for paper bag, **till the time** for "by the time," and **rainworm** for earthworm, from German **Regenwurm**. The Lehigh Valley and easternmost Berks County prefer **hoagie**, whereas Reading prefers **sub**. There is also a local term **Italian sandwich**, which during the 1960s was the primary term for a submarine sandwich in Reading and a secondary term in Allentown.

Harrisburg

In the 1939 surveys, Harrisburg made for an interesting contrast with Allentown and Bethlehem. Whereas there was a clear boundary and a steep dropoff of Philadelphianisms from Bucks and Montco north into the Lehigh Valley, there was instead a gradual tapering off of Philadelphianisms west toward the Susquehanna, making the boundaries much less clear. The Harrisburg and Lancaster areas typically showed a mix of both Philadelphia and Pennsylvania Dutch features, like **aow** alongside the standard **ow**; fronted *o* alongside monophthongal **o**, and long **a** pronounced as both diphthongal "eh-ee" and monophthongal **a**.

In the more recent data collected for the *Atlas of North American English*, Harrisburg agrees with Pittsburgh and Western PA in merging the short **oo** and long **oo** vowels before l: **full** (fool), **pull** (pool). Harrisburg also shows a continuous short **a** (n > d > g) system like Allentown, where short **a** is the most raised before **n**, and there is considerably more raising before **d**'s than **g**'s. Along with Western Pennsylvania the area uses **needs** + past participle (e.g. **needs washed)**, and **redd up** (clean up).

Down Jersey, Pine Barrens, and Delmarva

South Jersey—contrary to what is often stated—isn't uniformly part of the Philadelphia dialect area. The Pine Barrens, and the southernmost counties along Delaware Bay like Salem and Cumberland still hold on to a very Southern-sounding "Down Jersey" dialect that often surprises people when they hear it coming from a New Jersey native. Historically, this is the same dialect as Delmarvan across the Bay—a point which Kurath and McDavid themselves made in the last century, but which seems to have been generally forgotten.

In these areas **far** (fire) is merged with **far**. You'll also hear **arn** (iron) rhyming with **barn** and **carn** (corn)—in contrast to Philly where all three vowels are quite distinct: **iron/ahrn** (iron), **baurn** (barn), and **coorn** (corn). Down Jersey also has drawn-out Southern-style vowel sounds like **bayid** (bad), **weeyip** (whip), **feyince** (fence), and a few other oddities like **fawg** (fog) and **turkle** (turtle). Here Daniel Coye's survey also found **lahn** (lawn) with the vowel of "John."

Baltimore

The data collected for the *Atlas of North American English* did not show any substantial difference between Baltimore and Philadelphia, and for that reason scholars nowadays tend to group them together in a single MidAtlantic dialect.

But personally I believe this conclusion needs to be revisited. There is no question that the two dialects are very similar, but a thorough review of the available evidence from both scholarly and popular sources suggests some key distinctions.

As we've seen on page 13, glide deletion in **ire** is found to a limited degree in the Philly area. But while Philly does not go on to merge **fire** and **far**, this merger does apparently happen in Baltimore, as evidenced in Kurath and McDavid's *Pronunciation of English in the Atlantic States* (maps 46 & 47). The merger also appears in written Baltimorese as **arn** (iron), **far** (fire) far more often and less controversially than in Philadelphian. More than that, the Baltimore folk dictionaries suggest Southern-style glide deletion in far more contexts than I have ever seen hinted at in Philadelphian: **non** (nine), **tom** (time), **hah** (high), **quot** (quiet), **dod** (died), **lobble** (liable).

Additionally, we see a very different treatment of **oi**. Baltimorese has **awl** (oil), **jawn** (join), **bawl** (boil), and Aidan Malanoski in 2025 found the monophthongization of **oi** still present in Baltimore across racial groups. This change is particularly interesting because **oi** in Philadelphia goes in the opposite direction: not only keeping the glide but driving the **o** further forward in the mouth: **ooil** (oil), **jooyn** (join), **booyl** (boil).

Finally, the **r** in **warsh** (wash) is ubiquitous in the Baltimore folk literature but isn't typical of Philadelphia. Baltimore fully merges **Mary**, **marry**, and **merry** where Philadelphia keeps all three distinct, and Baltimore does not show the Philadelphian **er > ur** in words like **vurry** (very), nor does it make the word **crayon** monosyllabic and rhyme it with **crown**. In Baltimore **sub** is preferred over **hoagie**, and **creek** is used to the practical exclusion of **crick**. Positive **anymore** is not used in Baltimore city but does turn up elsewhere in Maryland, particularly along the Pennsylvania border and in Anne Arundel County. Likewise, Baltimoreans do not drop the prepositional object after **with** in sentences like **are you coming with?**

So notwithstanding the findings of the *Atlas*, it seems clear to me that Philadelphian and Baltimorese should be treated as closely related but still distinct dialects.

A Dictionurry a Phulladulphian

A

addytude   attitude. ***Aur spoorts faens gotta rully baed addytude.***

anyhal   anyhow.

anymoor   anymore; nowadays, currently (*can be used without a negative*): ***Things aur too expensive anymoor.***

aout   out. *Also spelled* **eowt.** ***Go aout and get yursulf some fresh air!***

al   ow! or owl. ***Al! I got clawed in the face by an al!***

a'er	hour. ***Da Iggles game starts in an a'er.***
apple taffy	a candied apple.
araound	around.
awf	off.
awfiss	office. ***Naow he's got his own awfiss!***
awl	all.
awn	on.
awr	are, our. ***Awr dose awrs? Yes dey awr!***
awruyt	all right, okay.

B

baby coach

An old local term for a baby carriage. *Very common throughout the Greater Philadelphia area in the first half of the 1900s but then declined in the second half of the century.*

baed

bad.

baen

band.

bag school

to skip school, play truant. *The earliest citations are from Camden around 1890; it was common in Philadelphia up to the mid-1950s but declined soon afterwards.*

baounce

bounce or balance. ***I caen't keep my baounce if you keep baouncin' awf me luyk at.***

beautyful

beautiful. ***Waow! You look beautyful, hon!***

beebee

baby.

beggle

bagel. ***Yizz wunt beggles fur breckfiss?***

boord board, bored.

boorn born. *Yeah, ruyt—I wasn't boorn yesturdy, ya know.*

booy boy.

bor bar. *I was hangin' aout at the bor laest nuyt.*

bork bark. *Is 'at daug rully gonna bork all nuyt?*

born barn. *Dat quooderback couldn't hit the side of a born door!*

boxball a game played with a large red ball, involving four squares drawn onto the ground and in which players try to eliminate others by bouncing the ball inside their square.

braln brown. *Da Skook'l's lookin braln lately.*

brooyl broil. *Maen, I'm brooylin' innis heat!*

buck-buck a game popular in the mid-1900s in which teams of boys jump on the backs of their opponents.

buhll

bell. [*this rhymes with* dull.] ***Wur gewin' daown ta see the Liburty Buhll.***

burry

berry, bury.

buyk

bike. ***Somebody stole my buyk ruyt aoutside my haouse!***

buyt

bite, a snack. ***Lemme get a buyt ta eat furst.***

C

caen
an (aluminum) or metal can. ***Gimme a caen a soda.***

caen't
can't. ***I caen't come in today...the shtreets are covered in uyce.*** *The final **-t** is not always pronounced, especially before words that begin with t, as in **Nope, I caen' tull 'er nothin'.** Note that although the noun **caen** and the negated **caen't** are always pronounced with a tense **a**, the verb **can** is pronounced with lax **a**.*

cal
cow.

calny
county. ***My uncle lives up in Mon'gumry Calny.***

calrie
cowrie; calorie. ***Hal many calries d'ya think are in calries?***

cawffee
coffee. ***If yur gehwin ta Wawa, can ya get me a cuppa cawffee?***

cenner
center. ***I saw yiz daown in Cenner City laest nuyt.***

chauk nuyt

1. the night before Mischief Night, or two nights before Halloween, 2. the night before Soap Night, two nights before Halloween.

chort

chart.

choor

chore. ***Aur you done yur choores?***

churry

cherry. ***My fav'rite wooder uyce is churry.***

claoud

cloud.

close

turn off, turn out: ***close da luyt.***

-co

abbreviation of county. *Seen in* **Chesco, Delco, Montco**.

cor

car.

cormul

caramel.

corpit

carpet.

cort

cart.

craln   crown, or crayon. ***Jus' give the kid a box a cralns.***

crick   creek. ***We useta gew ta Pennypack and play inna crick.***

D

da the.

daown down.

daownna down (to) the. ***Wur headin' daownna shoor this weekend.***

daowntaown downtown. ***Maen, the traffic was nuts daowntaown!***

dawg dog.

dem them.

dennis dentist.

dew do.

dewin doing. ***Wuddyiz dewin?***

dey they.

deze these.

dint did not, didn't.

dis   this.

doll   doll, dial.

dork   dark.

dorlin   darling.

dort   dart.

droor   drawer. *I caen' get this dorn droor open!*

dude   a performer in the Mummers' Comic Brigades dressed as a man.

dully   deli. *Meet me at da coorner dully fur lunch.*

E

easter mork

An obsolete term for a smashed egg on a brick wall, performed as a children's game during the Easter season.

enner

enter.

epper

an old-fashioned and probably now obsolete term for an Easter game in which opposing players tap two eggs together to see which cracks first. *Also* emper, upper.

expeck

expect.

exshtra

extra.

F

fal   foul, fowl.

faown'in   fountain.

faound   found.

fie   five: fie dollers.

fiff   fifth. *Also* **fit**.

flaowur   flower, flour.

fleas   Phillies.

fluffya   Philadelphia. *This is the most common way to write the city's name in dialect, going back at least to 1975. In a 1983 interview with Jim Quinn, linguist Bill Labov said of Fluffya: "Whoever invented that spelling...should get the Nobel Prize. It's perfect."*

fluffyan   Philadelphian. *Also* **Filufyan.**

fol   file. ***All a yiz need to line up single fol***.

foor   four.

foorty　　forty.

foork　　fork.

for　　far.

form　　farm.

formur　　farmer.

fren　　friend.

furrit　　ferret. *My niece got a pet furrit.*

furry　　ferry, furry. *We took the furry ta Caemdin.*

fuyt　　fight. *Dem Broad Shtreet Bullies rully knew haow ta fuyt!*

G

gaez gas. *I gotta stop an get gaez.*

gawna going to.

gehwin going. *Wair yiz gehwin?*

glaed glad. *O'm glaed yiz were able ta make it tanuyt.* *This is one of the few raised short **a** words that end with **d**.*

goorgeous gorgeous.

gordin garden.

graddyfy gratify.

graddytude gratitude. *Is a little graddytude too much ta aesk?*

gral growl. *I wuz waukin' paest a haouse and thur dawg staurted ta gral.*

graoun ground. *Jus' put it aunna graoun!*

H

haen   hand.

haouse   house.

hal   howl; how. ***Hal yiz dewin?***

hoagie   a submarine sandwich. Also **hoggie, hogie, hogey**. *Much has been written about this word, but its origins are still debated. Some popular theories are that it comes from "hoggie": either Hog Island Shipyard, or the ingredients or shape of the sandwich—and some early spellings of "hoggie" are believed to support this theory. Derivations have also been suggested from Hogan, hoke (a slang term used of hoboes), honky, and hookey. None of these latter seem very plausible; more likely are the competing claims of various restaurant owners. The first documented instance is in 1940, for a Sandwich Shop selling "steaks and hoggies" on West Passyunk Ave.* **Hogie** *was the common spelling through the 1940s, until* **hoagie** *surpassed it around 1950.*

hoagiemaouth   an affectionate nickname for the Philadelphia dialect, or a person who speaks it. *This is a relatively new term that seems to be from the early 2000s. Also spelled as two words:* **hoagie mouth**.

hoagie shop

an establishment where hoagies are sold; sandwich shop. *Commonly* **hogie shop** *in the 1940s.*

hole

hold.

holly

holly, highly. **He sez the Flyers have a chaence this year, but that's holly unluykly.**

hoorse

horse.

hord

hard.

hort

heart.

hull

hell.

hulp

help. **Little hulp?** *was a very common phrase we heard growing up, when a ball gets away from the players and rolls toward someone who is not playing. It's obviously a simple request for a little help, but in context it basically means "can you throw the ball back over here?"*

hunner   hunter.

hunnerd   hundred.

huy chair   high chair. **See huy school below**.

huyk   hike. **Take a huyk, buddy!**

huy school

high school. **We went to the same huy school.** *Generally Philadelphians only raise their long **i**'s in the middle of a word, not at the end. So Philadelphians pronounce high as "hah-ee" in Junior High. So then why do we say **huy school**? Linguists theorize this phrase is an exception to the general rule because people have interpreted it as a single compound word, as if it were highschool. The same, probably, goes for a baby's **huy chair.***

I

iggle eagle. *'Memmer when we used ta go see the Iggles at the Vet?*

inna in the.

indypendince independence. *Also* **innapennence**. *Wur gewin' daown ta Indypendince Haul with aur histurry claess.*

indypendint independent. *Fur an ulderly lady, she's proody indypendint!*

inhurrit inherit.

innerest interest.

instytute institute.

invenner inventor.

invuyt invite.

irish potato

a coconut cream candy rolled in cinnamon and shaped like a small potato, popular around St. Patrick's Day.

itsulf

itself.

J

jabip — a fictional far-away place. *He lives aout in Jabip.* A city variation is **fith an Jabip.**

jawn — a thing. **Haen' me dat jawn!**

jimmies — bits of flavored candy sprinkled on ice cream; sprinkles. **I oweze put rainbow jimmies on my uyce cream.**

joolry — jewelry.

jooyn — join. **I hear he's jooynin da Iggles nex year.**

jor — jar. **Opennis jor foor me, willya?**

jully — jelly. **Ya wunna peanut butter an jully saenwich?**

jullyfish — jellyfish. **I was at Wahlwood an' got stung by a jullyfish.**

juvenahl — juvenile. **Dat kid is a juvenahl delinquint!**

K

kinnygaurden
kindergarten.

kurrosene
kerosene.

kuyt
kite.

L

laen land.

laenmaurk landmark.

laoud loud.

leaves aout lets out, gets out: *school leaves aout at three*.

lig league. *The Phils play in the National Lig.*

liggle legal. *Wut da mare is dewin' caen' be liggle!*

loord Lord. *Loord have murcy!*

looyer lawyer.

lorge large.

luyf life.

luyk   like. ***Hal can ya luyk mayo awn yur hoagie??!!***

luyt   light.

luytnin bug

the lightning bug or firefly.

lyburry   library.

M

mac an ATM or automated teller machine. *Also* **mac machine,** *and with derivatives such as* **mac card** (ATM card), **tap mac** (to withdraw from an ATM), *and* **hit the mac machine** (visit the ATM). *The MAC (Money Access Center) network was a creation of Philadelphia National Bank in 1979 and used by over a dozen other local banks. Its market share and prominent logo displayed on ATMs led to the network name being used as a common term. MAC as a brand was phased out after a merger in 2001, but by then the name was well entrenched locally as a common noun. it continues to be used to this day.*

maed mad.

mahoff a big shot, important person. ***He was the big mahoff of the block.***

mare mayor.

marelty mayoralty.

maoun'in mountain. ***In winner, we oweze go skiin' at Blue Maoun'in.***

malth mouth.

| **mawl** | mall. ***Wur headin ta King a Prusha Mawl.*** |

| **meanwol** | meanwhile. |

| **meer** | mirror. |

| **mennal** | mental. |

| **mischif nuyt** | the night before Halloween, on which pranks are sometimes performed. |

| **mol** | mile. ***He lives a mol daownna road from me.*** |

| **moor** | more. |

| **moornin** | morning, mourning. |

| **moorul** | moral. |

| **mork** | mark. |

| **morkit** | market. ***We're gonna get lunch at da Italian Morkit.*** |

| **morshmulla** | marshmallow. |

mullidy   melody.

Mummers   the Mummers' Parade, a New Year's Day folk tradition in Philadelphia featuring ornate costumes, string band music, and choreographed routines. Also refers to the people who participate in this event.

murry   merry. ***Yiz aull have a murry Chrismiss!***

muyt   might. ***I muyt jist take ya up awn 'at awffer.***

myin   mine, esp. when used for emphasis: ***Yo, don' take dat...it's myin!***

N

nal	now.
nao	no.
noorth	north.
nuyce	nice.
nuyf	knife.
nuyt	night, knight.
nyew	new.
nyewsy	nosy, not minding one's business.

O

oamost	almost.
oltnao	I don't know.
oor	or.
oordinurry	ordinary.
oorghin	organ. *We took the kids daownna Macy's ta hear the Wanamaker's oorgin.*
ooyl	oil.
ooyster	oyster.
open	turn on: open da luyt.
oweze	always. *He's oweze tryin' ta get me in trouble!*

P

paound pound.

paower power.

paymint sidewalk.

paymint bawl

a game like tennis played with the hands on the sidewalk.

peggin pagan.

pepper pot a typically Philadelphian soup made with tripe.

ph f. *It's the same sound either way, of course, but using ph's for f's is often seen in local sports writing (e.g. **Philly phans**) and cultural events. Washington Post sports columnist Ken Denlinger of Drumore, PA went all out with this passage in 1974: "These are phantastic, phabulous days for Philadelphians, the Veterans Stadium score board insists. The phightin' Phils are in phirst place, phinally; the phickle phans are phreindly. And the phuture seems promising, especially since the Phillies need not be overwhelming to win* *a championship but merely less phallible than the other phive clubs in the National League East.”*

Phanatic the beloved furry green mascot of the Phillies, who first appeared in 1978 as a replacement for the Bicentennial mascots Phil and Phillis. **Phanatic** *is actually an old form of "fanatic" cited in John Ash's 1775 English dictionary as a correct but uncommon spelling. So there.*

Philadelphese

The Philadelphia dialect. *This word is not very common but it does appear in print occasionally.* Also **Philadelphiaese.**

Phulladulphia Philadelphia. *This is my favorite version and the one closest to the way I say it— but there are many different variations like* **Phuldulfyeh, Fuldulphya**. *The most common by far is* **Fluffya**, *which first appeared in the 1970s.*

pitcher picture.

plaenner planner, planter.

plegg plague. ***Jimmy's actin' luyk he's got the friggin' plegg.***

pleece   police.

plenny   plenty.

pockabook   purse, handbag. ***We gotta go back, I lef' my pockabook at home.***

pol   pile. ***Pick up dat pol a cloze ya left aunna floor!***

poor   pore, poor.

poorch   porch.

poork   pork. ***I could rully go for a roast poork sanwich.***

poort   port.

pordy   party.

pork   park.

port   part.

praoud   proud.

prinner   printer.

proody   pretty. ***This rhymes with "woody".***

prostytute   prostitute.

pruyce   price.

puyk   pike.

puyp   pipe.

Q

quooder quarter.

quooder of a quarter till (the hour). ***We don't gotta leave till a quooder of.***

quooderback quarterback.

quoort quart.

quull quell.

quuyt quite.

R

raddyator   radiator.

raowdy   rowdy.

raound   round.

raout   rout.

razburry   raspberry.

rebaoun   rebound.

repoort   report.

riggle   regal. ***Haow 'about we catch a movie at the Riggle?***

road   way, path: ***Yo, I'm tryin ta get through here, get aoutta da road!***

rol   rile.

romaennic   romantic.

rullic   relic.

rullitive   relative.

rullivint   relevant.

ruyce   rice.

ruyder   writer.

ruyfle   rifle.

ruyp   ripe.

ruyt   right, write.

S

saen   sand.

saoun   sound.

salth   south. Also **sailth**.

sawf pretzel   a soft, baked pretzel sprinkled with salt crystals, formerly sold by street vendors.

scal   scowl.

scaout   scout.

scoor   score. ***Don't tull me the scoor! I haven't seen the game yet!***

scor   scar.

scorlit   scarlet.

scrapple   a local breakfast dish made with pork leftovers and cornmeal, sliced thin and fried. ***Yo, come awn oaver! Mom's makin' scrapple fur brekfiss!***

seen	saw, have seen: ***He ain't lyin...I seen it happin!***
semi-sixers	Seventy-Sixers.
shaower	shower. *Also* **sha'er**. *This is pronounced with a lax short **a**, as if you were saying "shatter" without the **t**.*
shooda	should have.
shoor	shore. **The Shoor** *with a definite article refers to the Atlantic coast of New Jersey. This term is ubiquitous in Pennsylvania and southern New Jersey, but Delawareans call their seaside locations* **beaches**.
shoort	short.
shooter	another name for a Mummer, participant in the Mummers' Parade.
shork	shark. ***Kids get ta touch shorks at da Caemdin Aquairyum.***
shorp	sharp.
shtrawburry	strawberry.

shtreet	street.

shtring baend

a typically Philadelphian musical ensemble consisting of banjos, saxophones, bowed strings, and glockenspiels. ***My buddy plays in a shtring baen'.***

shtrut	the typical Mummers' dance, performed with high stepping and bent knees, while the dancer leans his torso slowly back and forth and lifts his arms to the music. Frequently danced at local weddings.

shtruyk	strike.

shtruyp	stripe.

shulf	shelf.

shull	shell.

shulter	shelter.

shurriff	sheriff.

sixt	sixth.

sluyce slice.

smearcase cottage cheese.

smol smile.

smort smart.

smull smell.

snoor snore.

soda any carbonated soft drink.

soor sore, soar.

spaout spout.

spicket water faucet. ***Yo, turn on the spicket so I can wash my haens!***

splinner splinter.

spoort sport.

spork spark.

spraout sprout.

spull	spell (rhymes with dull).
spuyder	spider.
square	an old term for city block.
staen	stand.
stickbaul	a game similar to baseball but played with a broom handle and a tennis ball.
stol	style.
stoor	store.
stoorm	storm.
stoory	story.
stor	star.
stort	start.
storve	starve.
sturrul	sterile.
sulf	self.

sull   cell, sell.

sullur   cellar.

sullury   celery.

sullyular   cellular.

sum'n   something.

sundy   Sunday.

suyt   sight.

swoor   swore.

swul   swell.

swulter   swelter.

T

taower	tower.
taffy	lollipop.
tal	towel.
tamarra	tomorrow.
taown	town.
tap mac	to use an ATM machine, especially to withdraw cash. *See* MAC.
tawk	talk.
thur	they're. **Thur ovur at my haouse.**
tol	tile.
tole	told.
tollum	told him.
toor	tore.

toorch torch.

toord toward.

tral trowel.

traout trout.

trinity haouse

a type of rowhome consisting of three rooms stacked vertically, and characteristic city housing in the 18th century.

tull tell.

tullaphone telephone.

tullur teller.

tullypole telephone pole.

turnpuyk turnpike.

turror terror.

turrible terrible.

turritoory   territory.

tuydle   title, tidal. ***Maen', it wuz luyk a tuydal wave.***

tuyp   type.

tuyt   tight.

twulve   twelve.

twunny   twenty.

twuyced   twice.

U

ulbow	elbow.
ulderly	elderly.
ulf	elf.
ull	elevated train. ***Get awnna Ull at Girord.***
ulligible	eligible.
ullamint	element.
ullimennery	elementary. ***He's a fren a myin from ullimennery school.***
ulliphint	elephant.
ullivader	elevator.
ulm	elm.
ulse	else.
unnerstaen	understand.

urra   era. ***Dat was a great urra fur da Flyers.***

urrind   errand. ***He's aout runnin' an urrind.***

uyce   ice. ***Gew get me a bag a uyce.***

uytem   item.

V

val vowel. ***Pat, I'd luyk ta buy a val.***

vaouch vouch.

vegg vague. ***I don't know wut he's taukin' abaout..he's bein' kinda vegg.***

vol vile.

vurrify verify.

vurry very. ***It's vurry nuyce a ya ta say.***

W

wait up   wait a minute, hold it; wait for me.

wan   won: **Dey wan da game.**

wawk   walk.

wearat   where?

wen   when.

wench   a performer in the Mummers' Comic Brigades dressed as a woman.

wensdy   Wednesday.

wess   west.

wich   which.

wid   with. *In cheesesteak ordering,* **wid** *is short for* **with onions**.

widaout   without.

widges   with you (pl).

PARKINSON'S

FASHIONABLE CONFECTIONARY,

AND ICE CREAM SALOONS,

180 CHESNUT ST.

These *Spacious* and *Magnificent* Saloons are open during the day and evening for the reception of Visitors.—Coffee, Chocolate, Teas, Jellies, and a great variety of Cream and Water Ices supplied at a moment's notice.

ALWAYS ON HAND, a great variety of Bonbons, Christmas Toys, and Fancy Confectionary, selected at Paris expressly for the sales of this establishment.

N.B. ORDERS FROM ANY PART OF THE UNITED STATES for Preserved Fruits in Sugar or Brandy, Sugar Almonds, French, Italian, and Martinique Liquors, Candy and Confectionary in general, attended to with promptness and punctuality.

JANE WOOD'S

UNRIVALLED CONFECTIONARY,

AND ICE CREAM SALOONS,

187 Chesnut-St.,

Opposite the Hall of Indipendence.

Coffee, Chocolate, Cakes, Bonbons, and various kinds of Pastry, Ice Creams, Water Ices, Jellies, Brandied and Preserved Fruits.—Also Candies and all kinds of confectiontionary constantly on hand, and at the shortest notice.

MRS. WOOD most respectfully solicits the patronage of the Ladies and Gentlemen of the city of Philadelphia, and Strangers.

Her Coffee, Ice Cream, and Promenade Saloons, (particularly the Ladies' Saloons fronting in Chesnut street,) are second to none in this city. And the variety and excellence of her stores—the obliging demanor, promptness, and skill of those in attendance.—The eligible situation of her establishment, being directly in front of one of the most beautiful as well as one of the most fashionable promenades in the Union, renders her establishment, both for grave and gay, one of the most desireable places of resort.

Two Philadelphia confectionaries advertising "water ices" in A.E. Wright's Boston, New York, Philadelphia, & Baltimore Commercial Directory and General Advertising Medium (1840).

wifty

somewhat eccentric; dim, absent-minded.

winda

window.

winecha

why don't you?

winner

winter.

wit

along: *Yo Tommy! Ya comin wit?*

wol

while.

wooder

water. *The classic Philly pronunciation of this is* **wooder**, *but some may say* **wutter**, **waudder**, *or* **wahder**.

woodermullon

watermelon.

wooder uyce

fruit juice, water, and syrups blended and frozen. **Nuthin' beats a churry wooder uyce aun a hot day.** *Water ices appear in English cookbooks in the 1780s, and were advertised by Philadelphia confectionaries since at least 1840 (see image on the previous page). Our local dialect has simply preserved a common English term that fell out of use elsewhere.*

woodevur   whatever.

woor   war, wore.

woord   ward.

woorm   warm.

woorn   warn.

wootna   wouldn't have.

wuhll   well (*rhymes with* dull).

wulcome   welcome.

wult   welt.

wunna   want to.

wunst   once.

wunt   want. ***Ga head...get woodevur yiz wunt!***

wunt auff   to want to get off, *also used with prepositions* in and aout.

wunnid   wanted.

wuyf   wife.

wuyt   white.

wy   why. ***Wy ya even aeskin' me dat?***

Y

yizz   you, you all. ***Wen 'r yizz headin' aout?***

yizzle   you will.

yo   hey there; hello. ***Yo, wuddya dewin?*** *Also can mean* you're kidding; you're putting me on: ***Yo, come off it.***

yoomer   humor.

yoomid   humid.

yoomin   human.

yoor   your.

yord   yard. ***He's aout playin' inna yord.***

youse   you plural, you all; *some speakers also use this for singular you. Also* **yuze**. *This pronoun, once common through much of the Northeast and Midwest, has long been stigmatized as lower class. It is still used but appears to be declining in favor of* **you guys.**

yuge	huge.
yull	yell.
yulla	yellow.
yumid	humid.

Z

zep A local sandwich from Norristown, similar to a hoagie but with cooked salami and no lettuce. *Also* **zeppelin**.

zink sink.

zullus zealous.

Places Ta Gew

Ahlanee — Olney. *Also* **Awlney**.

Cenner Ciddy — Center City. *Also* **Senda Ciddy**.

Chesco — Chester County

Ciddy Haw — City Hall

Conshy — Conshohocken

Dulco — Delaware County

Eas Fawls — East Falls.

Fairmaount Pork — Fairmount Park.

Gimty — Germantown

Hunning Pork — Hunting Park

Innypennense Hawl — Independence Hall. *Also* **Innapenn-ense Hawl**.

King a Presha — King of Prussia

Laocuss Shtreet — Locust Street

Manneeyunk — Manayunk

Montco — Montgomery County

Noorfeass — Northeast Philadelphia

Passhunk — Passyunk

Pensuhvaynyuh — Pennsylvania

Penn's Laenning — Penn's Landing

Saouff Fluffya — South Philadelphia. *Also* **Sout Filufya**.

Saouf Shtreet — South Street. *Also* **Sout Shtreet**.

Shel'nhaem — Cheltenham.

Skook'l — Schuylkill.

Somer'n	Somerton.
Two Shtreet	Second Street.
Vilnoava	Villanova.
Wall Women Bridge	Walt Whitman Bridge.
Wissahickin Crick	Wissahickon Creek.

Caemdin	Camden
Daownashoor	The New Jersey Shore
Lannick Ciddy	Atlantic City
OhCee	Ocean City
Treh'in	Trenton
Salth Jurzy	South Jersey
Wahwood	Wildwood

Al-in-taown	Allentown. *We could even say* **Owl-in-taown** *and no one would ever notice the difference.*
Pokenoes	Poconos
Noo Yoork	New York

Dullaware	Delaware. *Also* **Delawur**.
Woomingtun	Wilmington.
Baltymoor	Baltimore
Murralind	Maryland. *Also* **Murlin**.
Flaurda	Florida

Itly	Italy
Jabip	????

Ta Lurn Moor

I've tried to keep this book light and accessible for a general readership rather than cluttered with references, so it may seem like I have made some claims out of thin air. But I am currently working on a reference dictionary of the Philadelphia dialect that includes extensive historical citations for those who want a more scholarly presentation of the data, which I hope will be published in late 2026.

In the meantime, if you'd like to learn more about the Philadelphia dialect, here are some resources that may be helpful.

Clark DeLeon. 2001. "Do Pennsylvanians Tawk Funny?" in *Pennsylvania Curiosities: Quirky Characters, Roadside Oddities and other Offbeat Stuff.* Guilford, CT:Globe Pequot Press.

Michael Lawrence Ellis III. 1993. *Philly Fun-ics: Now Yuze Can Talk Like Us.* Wayne, PA: Valley Forge Publishing.

Hans Kurath. 1949. *A Word Geography of the Eastern United States.* Ann Arbor: University of Michigan Press.

Hans Kurath and Raven I. McDavid. 1961. *The Pronunciation of English in the Atlantic States.* Ann Arbor: University of Michigan Press.

William Labov, Sharon Ash, and Charles Boberg. 2006. *The Atlas of North American English: Phonetics, Phonology, and Sound Change.* Berlin/New York: Mouton de Gruyter.

Dennis Lebofsky. 1970. *The Lexicon of the Philadelphia Metropolitan Area.* PhD dissertation, Princeton University.

Sean Monahan. 2010. Philly Tawk: A discussion awn Mid-Atlantic English...and other stuff. *http://phillytawk.blogspot.com/. And see also Sean's numerous YouTube videos on the subject.*

Jim Quinn. 1975. "How to Talk Like a Philadelphian", *Philadelphia Magazine,* 66:11, pp. 136-154 (November 1975).

Jim Quinn. 1976. "How to Talk Like a Philadelphian Part II", *Philadelphia Magazine* 67:3, pp. 124-127 (March 1976).

Jim Quinn. 1983. "Why we talk the way we do." *The Philadelphia Inquirer Magazine.* August 28, 1983, pp. 33-38.

Jim Quinn. 1997. "Phillyspeak." *Philadelphia City Paper.* August 14-21, 1997.

Claudio R. Salvucci. 1995. *A Grammar of the Philadelphia Dialect.* Bucks County, PA: Evolution Publishing.

Claudio R. Salvucci. 1996. *The Philadelphia Dialect Dictionary.* Bucks County, PA: Evolution Publishing.

Claudio R. Salvucci. 2006. "Expressions of Brotherly Love," in Walt Wolfram and Ben Ward, eds. *American Voices: How Dialects Differ from Coast to Coast,* pp. 88-91. Malden, MA: Blackwell Publishing.

R. Whitney Tucker. 1944. "Notes on the Philadelphia Dialect." *American Speech* 19:37-42.

R. Whitney Tucker. 1964. "More on the Philadelphia Dialect." *American Speech* 39:157-158